I Bet I Won't Fret

A Workbook to Help Children with Generalized Anxiety Disorder

TIMOTHY A. SISEMORE, PH.D.

Instant Help Books
A Division of New Harbinger Publications, Inc.

Distributed in Canada by Raincoast Books

Copyright © 2007 by Timothy A. Sisemore, Ph.D.
Instant Help Books
A Division of New Harbinger Publications, Inc.
5674 Shattuck Avenue Oakland, CA 94609
www.newharbinger.com

Cover design by Amy Shoup

Text design by David Eustace

Printed in the United States of America

Library of Congress Cataloging-in-Publication Data

Sisemore, Timothy A.
  I bet I won't fret / by Timothy A. Sisemore.
     p. cm.
  Includes bibliographical references and index.
  ISBN-13: 978-1-57224-600-3 (pbk. : alk. paper)
  ISBN-10: 1-57224-600-6 (pbk. : alk. paper)
  1. Anxiety in children--Problems, exercises, etc. I. Title.
RJ506.A58S57 2008
618.92'852200078--dc22

                                        2007051978

10   09   08

10   9   8   7   6   5   4   3   2   1

First printing

Table of Contents

A Note to Parents

We all experience anxiety at some time during our lives when confronted by difficult circumstances, but some children experience anxiety over everyday activities and events and this becomes a constant and pervasive condition. This workbook was designed to help children with generalized anxiety disorder or GAD. Typically children or teens who have GAD experi- ence excessive worry and fear about a number of concerns for a period of at least six months, along with an inability to control their worry. Some of these concerns may relate to real-life situations, such as problems in school, and others may be about unlikely or unrealistic things, like being hit by a meteor. Sometimes worry may be free-floating and not linked to a specific aspect of life. Children may simply feel anxious all of the time for no apparent reason.

Children with anxiety disorders will almost always benefit from seeing a professional counselor. Sometimes this can be for just a few months, and sometimes it can be for a longer period. This will, of course, depend on the seriousness of your child's problem with anxiety.

There are also a variety of medications that can help children with severe anxiety disorders, but these can only be prescribed after a thorough medical and psychological evaluation. Medication does not take the place of counseling, but it can help reduce the symptoms that interfere with a child's day-to-day functioning.

This workbook will provide you with activities that you can do at home that are similar to the ones that your child will learn in counseling. They will also give you insight on how best to help your child.

The activities in this book will teach your child to self-calm in the face of anxiety, identify and get rid of irrational thoughts, develop realistic problem-solving skills, and much more. These new thinking, emotional, and behavioral skills will help your child overcome his current symp- toms and develop better ways to cope for years to come.

Children learn emotional intelligence skills just like they learn academic or athletic skills: through practice and encouragement. Your child will likely need your guidance in going through this workbook, and he or she will certainly need your encouragement.

As you help your child, you will probably find out that it is difficult for him to talk about certain issues. Never force your child to talk if he doesn't want to. The best way to get children to open up is to be a good role model. Talk about your thoughts, feelings, and experiences as they relate to each activity, stressing the positive ways that you cope with problems. Even if your child doesn't say a thing back, your words will have an impact on his behavior.

There is no wrong way to use this workbook to help your child as long as you remain patient and respectful of your child's feelings. If you child is being seen by a counselor for his anxiety disorder, make sure you share this workbook with the therapist. He may have some additional ideas on how best to use the activities.

Anxiety disorders can be very difficult for children as well as their families. Your patience and understanding will make all the difference.

Sincerely,

Lawrence E. Shapiro, Ph.D.

Before You Begin

Hello there, my friend!

My name is Dr. Tim Sisemore, and I work with children who sometimes get nervous and worried. Someone who cares about you has given you this workbook because he or she thinks you would be happier if you worried a little less than you do right now. Most likely, you think so, too.

One reason I really like to work with kids who are anxious (a fancy word for worrying or being nervous) is that they are usually pretty eager to fight their worries and they work hard to do just that. And that means that very often they beat their worries ... or at least get to where they don't worry nearly as much as they used to.

Practice really helps. If you want to be a better piano player, baseball player, singer, or whatever, you have to practice, right? The idea for this book is to give you some activities that let you practice some things that will help you overcome your nervous feeling and thinking. I've tried to make the activities fun, but they still require a little work. Practicing isn't as much fun as winning the game or hearing people clapping after you've given a musical performance. But if you don't practice, you may not enjoy those good endings.

As you begin, imagine how great life would be if you weren't as nervous or worried as you are now. You'd feel better and would have more free time to do things that are a lot more fun than being nervous. That's the goal, and these activities are the "practice" that will get you to that goal. Once you beat the worries, you'll get to enjoy the good feelings for a long time ... the rest of your life!

So, with this exciting goal in mind, let's get started. Soon, when worry comes after you, you will be able to say, "No problem ... I bet I won't fret!"

> **Assignment:** Identify some things you would like to help motivate you in fighting your fears.

Let's face it. We all like to be rewarded. Just about everything we do is done to try to get something we'd like. You might like a new toy or your mom's praise or even just the good feeling of knowing your chores are done for the day.

Fighting worries can be hard work. So adding a reward to the good feeling of beating your worries can help.

In this activity, you are to go through the list of possible rewards and find the five that are most interesting to you. Rank them from 1 to 5, with the number "1" being the reward that you would like the most. Notice that there's a place to put in a reward of your own in case you think of one I missed.

If it's okay with your mom and dad, you should get one reward from this list for each activity in this book that you complete. Finally, talk with your parents and decide on a really great reward to celebrate when you finish the whole "I Bet I Won't Fret" program. Mark it down on the sheet so that you won't forget it.

- ☐ Buy a new book
- ☐ Buy a new CD, DVD, or video
- ☐ Candy: Name your favorite _____
- ☐ Choice of food for meals
- ☐ Computer time
- ☐ Favorite dessert: Name it _____
- ☐ Foods: Name three _____
- ☐ Free time
- ☐ Fruit: Name your favorite
- ☐ Go bowling
- ☐ Go to a ball game
- ☐ Go to the movies

- ☐ Go to the mall or shopping
- ☐ Go outside
- ☐ Have a friend come over
- ☐ Listen to music
- ☐ Money
- ☐ New toy: Name it _____
- ☐ No chores for a day
- ☐ Playdate with a friend
- ☐ Play with a favorite toy
- ☐ Play in the yard
- ☐ Play a favorite sport (shoot baskets, kick a soccer ball, and so forth)
- ☐ Ride a bicycle
- ☐ Snack: Name two favorites _____
- ☐ Spend the night with a friend or relative
- ☐ Stay up later at night
- ☐ Telephone time
- ☐ Time with your mom or dad
- ☐ Time with a friend
- ☐ Trip to a favorite restaurant: Name it _____
- ☐ Trip to a park
- ☐ Trip to a video arcade
- ☐ Video game time: Name your favorite _____
- ☐ Watch a video or DVD
- ☐ Watch a favorite TV show
- ☐ Name one we didn't think of _____
- ☐ And name a really nice one for when you finish the program:

  _____

Take Note

It's fun thinking of stuff you'd like to earn for a reward. But remember, one of the best things about doing the activities in this program is how good it's going to feel to beat your worries. You're going to really enjoy trading the time you spend worrying for doing more enjoyable things—and that's going to be your best reward!

Talk with your mom or dad, and work out little rewards for each activity you finish. Perhaps if you do 10 assignments, you'd get a little bigger reward instead of 10 little ones. Figure out your plan, and write it below.

Reward   **Number of Activities Required to Get It**

_____

_____

_____

_____

_____

_____

_____

Activity 2   The Anxious Aardvark

Assignment: Learn about another child who worries and see how much you have in common.

You're doing these activities because you believe, or someone who cares about you believes, you worry enough that it bothers you. Our first activity is for you to read about another child who has some of the same things happening. Doing this will help you understand more about how worries work and how you can get over them. It also helps a lot of kids to know that other kids know how they feel. So, reading this story may help you feel better about your worries. In this story you will read about an aardvark. Do you know what that is? It is a cute but funny-looking animal. Have you seen the cartoon of Arthur on TV? He is an aardvark, too.

Read the story two times or have someone else read it to you two times. The first time you read it, just learn about Taylor. Then read it again and think about how much you are like Taylor and how you are different from Taylor. Then tell your mom, dad, or another person who loves you what you learned.

The more we know about worrying, the better we can be at stopping it!

Once upon a time there was a young aardvark named Taylor. Taylor's family was like other aardvark families. They lived in a nice house and had some nice things. They loved Taylor, and Taylor loved them.

Taylor went to kindergarten at Aardvark Elementary School and had some good friends. But Taylor had a problem. Taylor worried and worried about some things.

"What if my mom forgets to pick me up after school? What if there is a tornado? What if I can't learn to read very well? What if I get into trouble and am punished? What if no one will play with me?"

Taylor's friends worried sometimes too. But Taylor worried more than everyone else. One day Taylor asked the teacher, Ms. Green, if she would be mad at him if he didn't color his picture very well. She said, "Taylor, you are really an anxious aardvark!"

"Ms. Green, what does 'anxious' mean?"

Ms. Green replied, "I'm sorry. That's kind of a big word. 'Anxious' means worried about stuff. You worry about what might happen and feel scared that something bad might happen."

"Oh," he said, "then I'm anxious a lot!"

Ms. Green talked to his parents about his worrying (his anxious thinking). They asked him about it, and he was happy they were so interested.

"I worry about a lot of things," he told his mom and dad. "I'm anxious about whether or not you will pick me up on time after school. I'm anxious about school and if Ms. Green thinks I'm smart. I'm anxious that there might be scary things in my closet at night."

He got to use his new word, "anxious," a whole lot that day!

His mom and dad told him that feeling anxious is why he was grumpy some days and why he didn't feel too well sometimes when he went to bed at night. (He didn't know worrying could make you feel funny, but it does!)

His dad took him to see another kind of teacher he called a counselor. He was one of the nicest aardvarks in town! He told Taylor that other children were anxious like he was and he told him some neat things he could do to help him stop worrying and being anxious.

Taylor still worries sometimes, but not very much. His counselor really helped him. So did his mom and dad and Ms. Green. He is really glad he's not so anxious anymore.

Do you worry a lot like Taylor did? Then talk to your parents or teacher. A counselor can help you, too. All you have to do is try the things you talk about. These things help aardvarks … and they help human kids, too!

Take Note

Describe Taylor in your own words.

_____

_____

_____

What are the things about Taylor that let you know Taylor worries?

_____

_____

_____

What are some ways you are like Taylor?

_____

_____

_____

What are some ways you are not like Taylor?

_____

_____

_____

Write one main thing you learned in this activity about worrying.

_____

_____

_____

Activity 3   "I Bet I Won't Fret"

> **Assignment:** Learn about another child who worries and see how much you have in common.

You're working on this workbook because either you or someone who cares about you believes you worry too much.

In this activity, you'll read about another child who may have some of the same things happening in his life as you do.

This story may help you understand more about how worries work and how you can get over them. It helps a lot of kids to know that there are other children just like them. So, reading this story may help you feel better about your worries. Oh, and in case you don't know, "fret" is just another word for worry.

Read the story two times. The first time you read it, just learn about Robin. Then read it again and think about how much you are like Robin and how you are different from Robin. Then tell your mom, dad, or another person who loves you what you learned.

Hey! My name is Robin. I'm in the fifth grade at Franklin Elementary and I enjoy music and soccer. I have one older brother and a naughty little sister. We live with our parents in a nice house and have a pretty happy life … except for one problem: I worry a lot. Oh, I know, everybody worries sometimes, like if you have to speak in front of the class or if your grandma's really sick. But I worry a whole lot.

I worry about the normal types of things but I worry about them too much. If I have a spelling test, I don't just study.… I worry about it all week, study every night, and have trouble sleeping the night before I take it. If one of my friends says something to me like, "Your hair looks funny today," I start worrying about what is wrong with my hair. Most kids would think about this for a minute or two, but I might fret about it for a whole week, and I start wondering if my friend doesn't like me, and what is wrong with me, and will I ever have any good friends, and so on.

But I also worry about things most kids don't even think about. If my mom says I can't get a new CD I want, I start worrying that maybe we don't have enough money and that we might have to move out of our house, or we might go broke or not have food.

Part of me knows that's silly, but I think that way a lot. For example, my dad came home one day and said that we were going to eat at a new restaurant. My brother and sister got excited, but I got nervous. I thought: "What will it look like? What kind of food will they have? Will I like it? Will it be scary?"

I get so upset sometimes that I feel sick to my stomach and then don't want to eat.

That's the other thing. My worrying makes me feel funny sometimes. I feel sick to my stomach almost every day. I don't sleep too well sometimes and I get jumpy every time I hear a little noise. When I'm worrying, I get grumpy and grouchy, and that gets me in trouble sometimes. What I worry about changes, but what doesn't change is that I worry. I didn't like to talk about it, because I also was afraid something was wrong with me.

Finally, my mom talked to me and said she knew I worried a lot. She said she knew that worrying wasn't much fun and was making me feel bad a lot. I liked that she understood how I felt. But then she made me really worried.... She told me she was taking me to a counselor. "Oh, no! She thinks I'm crazy," I thought. But she took me anyway.

I'll never forget how nervous I was at that first visit. I even promised my dad I'd never worry about anything again if they would just take me home. But they didn't. My counselor was actually a nice lady who said she had talked to other kids who worry a lot and that this is a common problem. That was cool to hear because I thought nobody worried like I do. She said she could teach me some tricks that would help me not to worry. She got me to believe that if I practiced the things we worked on, I could say, "I bet I won't fret" and I wouldn't.

Well, it worked! Oh, I still worry sometimes, but I don't think I worry more than most kids. It was a little scary to talk to my counselor at first, but now I think she is pretty special.

So I hear maybe you have some worry problems, too. And you have to talk to a counselor like I did. Hey, take it from me. Now I know when something could worry me, I can say, "I bet I won't fret," and I don't. And I bet before long you won't either!

Take Note

Describe Robin in your own words.

_____

_____

_____

What are the things about Robin that let you know Robin worries?

_____

_____

_____

What are some ways you are like Robin?

_____

_____

_____

What are some ways you are not like Robin?

_____

_____

_____

Write one main thing you learned about worrying in this activity.

_____

_____

_____

Activity 4   Things I Worry About

> **Assignment:** Find out what things you worry about
> and how much you worry about them.

If we're going to learn how to worry less, we need to learn more about what we worry about. Then we will have a better idea of what we need to work on. It also helps if we know what things we worry about the most. That helps us know what things will need the most work. So, let's look at our next activity.

You may want to make copies of the Things I Worry About sheet as we will use it often. The first time it will let us know how bad the worries are to start with. Then, you can fill it out again and see how you're doing as you learn how not to fret.

You can also let your parents fill out a copy. Then you can compare what you think you worry about with what they think you worry about. That does not mean one of you is right or wrong, just that you've noticed different things. Having more people help only means you can do a better job of beating the worries.

Name _____ Age _____ Date _____

How much do you worry about these things?

	None	A Little Bit	Pretty Much	A Whole Lot
Being alone	_____	_____	_____	_____
Being in a big crowd	_____	_____	_____	_____
Being on time for school	_____	_____	_____	_____
Changes in my schedule	_____	_____	_____	_____
The dark	_____	_____	_____	_____
Flying on an airplane	_____	_____	_____	_____
Being with my friends	_____	_____	_____	_____
Getting embarrassed	_____	_____	_____	_____
Getting kidnapped	_____	_____	_____	_____
Getting lost	_____	_____	_____	_____
Getting hurt	_____	_____	_____	_____
Having to wear certain clothes	_____	_____	_____	_____
Getting in trouble	_____	_____	_____	_____
Getting sick	_____	_____	_____	_____
Going to bed alone	_____	_____	_____	_____
Going to new places	_____	_____	_____	_____
High places	_____	_____	_____	_____
How good I am at the things I do	_____	_____	_____	_____
How I look	_____	_____	_____	_____

How many friends I have   _____ _____ _____ _____

How much money we have   _____ _____ _____ _____

Looking foolish   _____ _____ _____ _____

Loud noises   _____ _____ _____ _____

Monsters or ghosts   _____ _____ _____ _____

My parents forgetting me   _____ _____ _____ _____

My parents getting a divorce   _____ _____ _____ _____

My grades   _____ _____ _____ _____

News I see on TV   _____ _____ _____ _____

Not being able to breathe   _____ _____ _____ _____

Riding on a bus or in the car   _____ _____ _____ _____

Robbers   _____ _____ _____ _____

Schoolwork   _____ _____ _____ _____

Something bad happening to my   _____ _____ _____ _____
parents

Storms or tornadoes   _____ _____ _____ _____

Terrorists or war   _____ _____ _____ _____

Tests   _____ _____ _____ _____

Take Note

What three things do you worry about most?

_____

_____

_____

What three things did your parent think you worry about most?

_____

_____

_____

Now that you think of it, was your parent correct about anything he or she noticed that you really had not noticed?

_____

If you could get rid of one worry, which one would it be?

_____

How would your life be better if you didn't have that worry?

_____

_____

_____

_____

If you have filled out the Things I Worry About chart before, which worries are better this time?

_____

Are any of your worries worse than last time?

_____

Activity 5 — Stresses in My Life

Assignment: Learn about other things going on that might make your worries stronger.

There is, of course, a difference between real worries and those that aren't so real. If someone you love gets hurt and goes to the hospital, that's a real worry. Something bad really happened, and you're not sure how it will turn out.

Most worries are not so real. For example, you might worry about getting hit by a tornado. Yes, that might happen, but it's almost certain that it won't. Very few people ever even see a tornado, much less are in one.

These worries are tricky because they probably won't happen, but you know they could. Learning not to worry will mean not letting these not-so-real worries get to you. But it's harder to work on these when there are real things that worry and stress you.

The next assignment gives you a list of these real worries that might make more stress and worry in your life. The more of these things you have in your life, the more likely it is that worry and stress will bother you. It's important to know this so that you understand the things that could make your worries worse.

Mark the sheet on the next page to find out what real worries are affecting your life. These are things that have been going on during the past year.

Check all the things that apply to your life over the past year.

☐ One of my grandparents died. (3 points)

☐ One of my parents was very sick for a long time. (3 points)

☐ My parents divorced. (4 points)

☐ My parents decided to live apart. (4 points)

☐ My parents divorced a long time ago but continue to argue about stuff. (3 points)

☐ My family moved to a new city. (3 points)

☐ My family moved to a new house. (2 points)

☐ I moved to live with a different family member. (3 points)

☐ I changed schools. (2 points)

☐ I started having more trouble in school than I used to. (1 point)

☐ I was pretty sick, hurt, or in the hospital. (3 points)

☐ One of my brothers or sisters was pretty sick, hurt, or in the hospital. (2 points)

☐ My family is having to live on less money than we used to, or one of my parents lost his or her job. (2 points)

☐ I had a pet die. (2 points)

☐ I had a good friend move away or stop being my friend. (1 point)

☐ We had a baby born in the family. (2 points)

☐ We had one of my grandparents or someone else come to live with us. (2 points)

☐ There has been a lot more fussing in our house. (2 points)

☐   One of my parents started traveling as part of their job. (1 point)

☐   One of my family members or I was in a serious car accident. (2 points)

☐   I saw something really scary, like someone get hurt badly, a wreck, or an explosion. (2 points)

There may be some smaller things that have stressed you, too.
Please list these below:

1. _____

2. _____

3. _____

4. _____

5. _____

Add all the points on the things you checked. Add one point for each thing you added at the end. Put the number below.

TOTAL POINTS : _____

Rate your stress like this:

0-3 points	Mild stress
4-8 points	Moderate stress
9-12 points	Serious stress
More than 12 points	Very serious stress

What does my score mean?

The more serious your stress, the more real the worries you have. When you have more real worries, it makes it harder to sort the real from the not-so-real worries. Maybe your counselor and parents can help you with that.

If you have a whole lot of stress, it is important to do some things to help with it. Some things you can do include:

Talk to your parents

Talk to a friend Get more exercise Get more rest

Write in a diary or journal

Draw pictures that express feelings

Write other things that might help below:

_____

_____

_____

_____

_____

_____

Activity 6

How Anxious Am I?
The Nervous Thermometer

Assignment: Learn how to rate how nervous you feel.

How can you know when you feel less worried? In this activity, you will learn how to measure how upset you are when you are worrying. This will help you, your parents, and your counselor know how upset you feel when you are nervous. It will also help everyone tell when things aren't upsetting you as much. That way, you and those who care about you can tell when you are learning not to be so upset when you think about nervous things.

You may want to make some copies of this activity sheet so you can practice using it.

Use the Nervous Thermometer like a real thermometer, except for the part about putting it in your mouth! Just look at the numbers and decide which is most like the way you feel. If this is a little confusing, just ask someone who cares about you to help you decide. With a little practice, you'll get the hang of it!

I Bet I Won't Fret

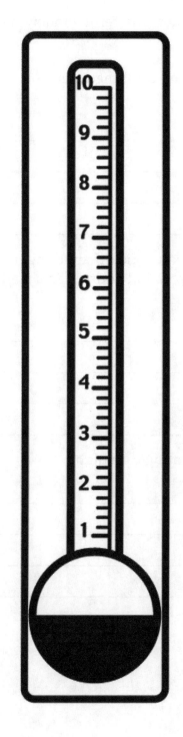

10. Really, really nervous. Worrying a whole lot, feeling shaky or sick to my stomach. Afraid I might lose control of myself.

9. Really nervous and worrying a whole lot. Feeling a little shaky or sick to my stomach.

8. Starting to wonder if I can handle it. Worrying a whole lot, starting to feel a little sick.

7. Really worried, but not feeling sick just yet.

6. Pretty worried.

5. Medium worried, thinking about stuff a lot, but I feel like I can control it.

4. Getting worried but not too bad.

3. Thinking about some stuff but not really worried about it.

2. Thinking mostly about good stuff.

1. Not worried at all! Feeling really good!

Take Note

After you've used the Nervous Thermometer a few times, answer the following questions.

What new things did you notice about your feelings and thinking when you tried to rate them on the thermometer?

_____

_____

_____

_____

What was your highest rating? _____ What did you notice, if anything, that might help you make that rating lower the next time you find yourself in a similar situation?

_____

_____

_____

_____

What types of things do you think about when your ratings are high?

_____

_____

_____

_____

What types of things do you think about when your ratings are low?

_____

_____

_____

_____

How could the things you think about when your ratings are low be helpful when your ratings are high?

_____

_____

_____

_____

How Am I Doing?

> **Assignment:** Learn how to track your nervous feeling
> and thinking using the Nervous Thermometer.

In the last activity, you learned how to use the Nervous Thermometer. Now, it's time to put it to use in your day-to-day life. This activity has a ratings sheet for you to use to record the ups and downs of your worries and nervous feelings. Make several copies of this so you can do this more than one time.

Fill in the form at least one time per day, but also when you feel like you're doing really well at handling your worries or when you're having a kind of hard time with worrying. Use the Nervous Thermometer to get your rating score.

It helps to try to record your feelings at different times of day. During the first week, try to get a rating in the early morning, while you're at school (if you're in school this week), in the afternoon, and in the evening. You might even rate yourself when you're lying in bed, about to go to sleep.

A Record Sheet for Monitoring My Thinking and Feeling
(to be used with the Nervous Thermometer)

Day	Time	Rating	What I Am Doing	What I Am Thinking
SAMPLE				
Monday	4:00 P.M.	6	Just got home from my new school.	Worrying about spelling words for this week.

Take Note

After you fill out your first week of the How Am I Doing? activity sheet, imagine you are being interviewed for TV about your assignment. Please answer our reporter's questions.

Reporter: I'm talking with _____ (your name), who has become an expert in tracking nervous feelings with the Nervous Thermometer. Tell us, did you see a pattern that your feelings are better at one time of day than at another? If so, when do they seem to be more of a problem?

Write your answer here:

_____

_____

_____

Reporter: What did you find to be the thing that you worried about the most?

Write your answer here:

_____

_____

_____

Reporter: Interesting. Did you notice that you worried about this at any particular times of day or in certain types of situations?

Write your answer here:

_____

_____

_____

Reporter: Excellent. I know our viewers really appreciate hearing from you. I bet it won't be long until you've learned not to fret. You're doing great! Thank you!

Feelings Charades

Activity 8

Assignment: Practice recognizing how people express feelings so that you can better recognize your own.

Did you ever see someone that you could tell was sad, even though they didn't say a word? You could tell what they were feeling by their body language. People show feelings with their faces, bodies, and even their tone of voice. What's funny is we mostly do this without anyone telling us how to do it. This also means we can be showing feelings with our bodies and not even realize the feeling we're showing.

This means that sometimes we might be fretting and showing it with our bodies, but not even know it. It's really hard to stop doing something you don't even know you are doing, isn't it? So, this activity is made to help you practice recognizing the feeling you and others show with your body language.

The next page can be copied, cut out, and made into a deck of cards. You can play Feelings Charades with two or more people. The idea is to pick one card and act out the feeling on it without saying anything. Just use your face and body. The other person has 30 seconds to figure out what you are feeling. The person who guesses it gets a point. If she doesn't guess correctly, she doesn't get a point. Then trade places, taking turns until someone gets 10 points.

Play this several times and with different people. That will help you notice the different ways people show their feelings. It also will help you to pay more attention to the way you show your feelings.

If you don't know what some of these words mean, leave them out of your game. Or, better yet, get a parent or someone else to explain the word, and how and when that feeling is expressed. Have fun!

Happy	**Sad**
Afraid	**Brave**
Guilty	**Proud**
Shy	**Surprised**
Anxious	**Loving**
Angry	**Bored**
Joyous	**Depressed**

Take Note

Now that you've practiced Feelings Charades a bit, try these questions:

Which feeling do you think was the hardest to express without words?

_____

Which feeling do you think was the easiest to express without words?

_____

Name one feeling word that you understand better now that you've done this activity.

_____

Describe the expression on your face when you are worried.

_____

_____

_____

Describe what your body does when you are worried.

_____

_____

_____

Activity 9   My Anxious Moments

> **Assignment:** Learn the pattern of single worries.

You've been working hard on our activities and learning more about your worries. The more you know about them, the easier it is to beat them.

This assignment will help you pay special attention to one worry at a time. So, you may want to make a few copies of the Anxious Moments sheet on the next page.

Earlier, you kept up with all of your worries on one sheet. Now you'll learn to look at one at a time. Choose one of the bigger worries you marked on the Things I Worry About assignment. For one whole day, mark down every time you notice yourself worrying about this. For example, if you worry about tornadoes, write down every time you find yourself worrying about a tornado. This way, we'll learn how often you worry about these, what times may be worse, and where you often are when you worry. It is important to keep track of these all day until you fall asleep at night. Your mom or dad may help by reminding you if they notice you worrying when you haven't noticed it yourself.

Then, try another one of your worries another day. Keep doing this until you have one day done on all the bigger worries that bother you. Then you, your parents, and your counselor will have a better idea of how to help you beat these worries!

My Name: _____ **Date:** _____

Today's Worry: _____

Time	What Was I Doing?	Where Was I?
_____	_____	_____
_____	_____	_____
_____	_____	_____
_____	_____	_____
_____	_____	_____
_____	_____	_____
_____	_____	_____
_____	_____	_____
_____	_____	_____
_____	_____	_____
_____	_____	_____
_____	_____	_____
_____	_____	_____
_____	_____	_____

Take Note

Now that you've kept track of your anxious moments for a few days, think about these questions.

Were you right about which thing you worry about the most or did you find you worried about another thing more? If so, which thing did you worry about the most?

_____

Concerning any of the worries, did you notice that you tend to have that worry at certain times of day or in certain situations? Fill in the blanks below:

Worry #	Worst Time of Day	Worst Place
1.	_____	_____
2.	_____	_____
3.	_____	_____

Did you happen to notice any times of day or any places you went where you didn't seem to worry so much? Write them here:

_____

_____

Do you have any ideas about why you didn't worry so much then and there?

_____

_____

> ### *Assignment:* Describe an episode
> ### of your worries or anxiety.

We're working on understanding what you think and feel when you worry or get nervous. When something important happens, TV stations send a reporter to the scene to talk with people about what happened. This helps everybody understand it better. Your worries are important. Maybe no real TV stations will talk with you about them (and you might not want them to anyway!), but let's pretend as a way of thinking about them.

There are a couple of different ways you can do this activity. Maybe the most fun is for a parent or someone to ask you the questions while video- or audio-taping your answers. This would be a neat thing to look at or listen to later on. You could also just have someone else ask you the questions and write down your answers. Or you can just write down the answers yourself. Whatever way works best for you will be fine.

This is your on-the-scene reporter with WXYZ news. Today we're reporting on how it feels to worry, and we're delighted to be at the home of _____ (your name). Thanks for letting us talk to you. I think what you have to say will be really helpful for our viewers. First of all, how long do you think worrying has been a bother to you?

Write your answer here:

_____

_____

Reporter: And what seems to be the biggest thing you worry about?

Write your answer here:

_____

_____

Reporter: I see. That doesn't sound like much fun to me, either. What kinds of things do you say to yourself when you're nervous about that?

Write your answer here:

_____

_____

Reporter: Interesting. What kinds of feelings do you have when you're thinking like that?

Write your answer here:

_____

_____

Reporter: I've heard some kids also notice that they're shaky or they feel their hearts beating really hard or stuff like that when they're nervous. Have you experienced any of that kind of thing?

Write your answer here:

_____

_____

Reporter: Very good. I wonder, can you tell when you're starting to get nervous or worried, or does it take a few minutes before you realize what's going on?

Write your answer here:

_____

_____

Reporter: And what is the first thing you notice when you realize you're worrying?

Write your answer here:

_____

_____

Reporter: I see. What have you tried to do to make these feelings and thoughts go away?

Write your answer here:

_____

_____

Reporter: Do any of these help very much?

Write your answer here:

_____

_____

Reporter: Interesting. How long does it usually take for you to start to feel better?

Write your answer here:

_____

_____

Reporter: What have your parents said to you about this problem?

Write your answer here:

_____

_____

Reporter: That sounds good. And how does it feel after you've been worried and nervous and you get back to feeling normal again?

Write your answer here:

_____

_____

Reporter: Great. One last question, _____ (your name). Do you have any advice you'd give to other kids who worry a lot who may be watching this program? There are a lot of them, you know. Any advice?

Write your answer here:

_____

_____

Reporter: Excellent! That should be helpful.

That's it from here. Thanks again to _____ (your name) for sharing with us today. I know this has been a big help. Now back to the studio....

Take Note

I hope that this activity was fun.

Did it feel good or sort of funny to imagine talking about your worries?

_____

_____

_____

How would you like to hear from someone else who has the same problem?

_____

_____

_____

Would that help you or not?

_____

_____

_____

How come it would or would not be a help to you?

_____

_____

_____

Write one thing you learned as you did this activity.

_____

_____

_____

My Nervous Mountain

> **Assignment:** Track your thinking and feeling through a time of worry or anxiety.

We've done a number of different things to look at your worries and anxiety so that we can understand them better and put together a really good plan to help you with them. This activity will help you understand how you think and feel during the time you are worrying or feeling nervous.

You may want someone who cares for you to help you with this activity because it may be a little hard. But I do believe you can do it!

There are two ways to start. Fill out the next two pages just after you've had a nervous time, or if you can already remember a nervous time, you can use that to fill out these pages.

Fill in the steps on the Nervous Mountain with answers to the questions that are on the page. This should help you see how nervous times begin, what changes as your worries get worse, and how they get better and leave you entirely.

It's good to know that you can always come down from Nervous Mountain, even though it may not feel too good at the top!

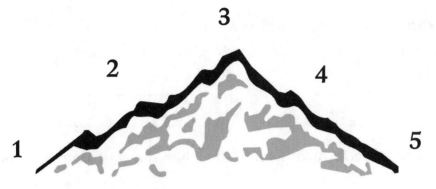

#1 Starting up the mountain

What are your first thoughts when you begin to be nervous?

_____

_____

_____

For some kids, there may be some uncomfortable feelings in your body before you notice you're worrying. What might these be for you?

_____

_____

_____

#2 Halfway up

How do your worries and feelings change when they start to get worse?

_____

_____

_____

#3 At the top

What are the feelings you have in your body when your worries are at their worst?

_____

_____

How does your body feel? Any different from when you started up the mountain?

_____

#4 Headed down

What is the first feeling to go away when you start to feel better?

_____

What helped your thinking to get better when your worries or nervousness were at their worst?

_____

_____

_____

#5 Back on level ground at last!

What are you thinking about now?

_____

_____

_____

How does your body feel? Any different from when you started up the mountain?

_____

Not a fun mountain to climb, huh? It's important to remember when you get upset with anxiety or worry that it DOES go away. That's good to know. So even when you're pretty unhappy with your worries, you can know they WILL get better.

Write down one thing you learned from climbing your Nervous Mountain.

_____

_____

_____

_____

_____

_____

Activity 12   My Anxiety Ladder

> ***Assignment:*** Rate your anxious times from easiest to hardest.

Wouldn't it be cool if you could just wave a magic wand and your worries would go away? It would be a lot easier than doing all these activities, wouldn't it?! But it doesn't work that way. The best way to beat the worries is to deal with them one at a time. What we hope to do is start with the smaller worries and work our way up to the big ones, knocking them out as we go.

The next exercise will help you plan how to do that. This is another exercise for which you may want a parent to give you a hand. There are two parts to this activity. First, think of as many situations as you can that worry you or make you nervous. For example, if you are scared of the dark, you might be a little nervous if you have to go upstairs by yourself in the daytime but more nervous if you have to go upstairs with the lights on at night. It might be a little worse still to be in your room with only a night light on. But it might be even worse if you have to stay in your room at night with no lights on at all! The idea is to think of the times, places, and thoughts that make you most nervous. Try to get at least 10. It's even better if you can think of 15.

Now, look through your list and figure out which one is the most upsetting. Put it at the top of the ladder with 100 points. Next, pick out the easiest one and put it near the bottom at … let's say … 10 points. This might be higher if this worries you more than just a little bit. Now, complete the rest of the ladder by placing all of your list in order from most upsetting at the top to least upsetting at the bottom.

My Nervous Times, Places, and Thoughts List

1. _____

2. _____

3. _____

4. _____

5. _____

6. _____

7. _____

8. _____

9. _____

10. _____

11. _____

12. _____

13. _____

14. _____

15. _____

Refer to the things you listed on the previous page and place them at the right place on the ladder. Something that makes you a little nervous would be low on the ladder, and something that makes you very nervous should be high on the ladder

100

90

80

70

60

50

40

30

20

10

0

_____

_____

_____

_____

_____

_____

_____

_____

_____

_____

_____

_____

_____

Take Note

Did you complete this activity? Way to go!

You should now have a good list to work from as you start taking on your worries. Feel free to change your ratings if a new worry comes along or one of them gets better or worse.

Meanwhile, write one thing you learned from doing this activity.

_____

_____

_____

_____

And try to think of one thing you could do to make the thing you worry about the least even lower on the scale:

_____

_____

_____

_____

Activity 13   Tense or Not?

> **Assignment:** Learn to notice nervous
> feelings in your body.

Some of the activities we've done have already asked you to start paying attention to feelings your body has when you are worried or nervous.

Did you know that our bodies send us signals all the time? We just don't usually pay very much attention to it when it does. Many kids who worry a lot have tensions and nervous feelings in their bodies, but not all of them. It is still helpful to learn to pay attention to your body, even if that's not been part of what troubles you.

In this exercise, you're going to practice learning to pay more attention to your body so you'll be better at catching nervous feelings. This will help you know when you're getting nervous, so you'll be able to stop climbing Nervous Mountain more quickly.

Practice the exercise once a day for a week. Try to notice something new each time you do it. Learning to pay attention to feelings in your body will help in lots of ways besides coping with anxiety.

This activity can be done on your own or with an adult reading the instructions to you. Find a chair with a back and arms on it. Have a seat and sit comfortably with your arms resting on the arms of the chair. Take a minute to relax. Try to breathe slowly and deeply. As you relax, start to notice any feelings you have in your body.

Start with your lower body. Can you feel your feet touching your shoes or the floor? Do you notice your legs pushing gently against the chair? Can you feel your bottom settling into the chair? Is it all comfortable, or do you notice any parts that don't feel very relaxed?

Now focus on to the middle of your body. Notice the relaxation of your muscles when you breathe out and the tension when you take a breath. Do you notice any tense spots? Can you hear your heart beating? You might even notice that it starts to beat more slowly as you become more relaxed.

Now pay attention to your arms. Notice the slight pressure as they rest against the arms of the chair. Can you feel anything else? Some kids may feel the air touching their skin, if they have on short sleeves, or the softness of fingers touching each other.

Now pay attention to your head and neck. Can you feel your head resting against the chair? Can you feel any of your hair touching your skin? Is your neck comfortable, or do you feel tension in it? What parts of your face do you notice? Is your mouth relaxed or tight? Can you feel your cheeks? What feelings do you have around your eyes?

Take one more minute. Can you notice any other sensations? Do you feel any changes in your feelings since you started the exercise?

Okay, nicely done. Take one or two more breaths, and then start to stretch. Slowly move your arms and head. Then you can get up … hopefully feeling more relaxed than when you started.

Do this five times during the week. Write down on the next page the feelings you notice each time.

#1 Day _____ Time I did my relaxation: _____

Feelings in my legs: _____

Feelings in my body: _____

Feelings in my arms: _____

Feelings in my neck and head: _____

#2 Day _____ Time I did my relaxation: _____

Feelings in my legs: _____

Feelings in my body: _____

Feelings in my arms: _____

Feelings in my neck and head: _____

#3 Day _____ Time I did my relaxation: _____

Feelings in my legs: _____

Feelings in my body: _____

Feelings in my arms: _____

Feelings in my neck and head: _____

#4 Day _____ Time I did my relaxation: _____

Feelings in my legs: _____

Feelings in my body: _____

Feelings in my arms: _____

Feelings in my neck and head: _____

#5 Day _____ Time I did my relaxation: _____

Feelings in my legs: _____

Feelings in my body: _____

Feelings in my arms: _____

Feelings in my neck and head: _____

Take Note

Write down three feelings you noticed as you did this activity that you had not noticed before:

_____

_____

_____

Write down one thing that you found helped you to relax as you did this activity:

_____

_____

_____

How did you feel different after the exercise than you did before it?

_____

_____

_____

Activity 14   The Story of My Life

> **Assignment:** Learn to imagine your
> life with fewer worries.

One of the cool things about being a kid is that you're still changing quite a bit and have a lot of growing to do. Did you ever imagine yourself as an adult? Maybe you've pretended to be a football player or movie star or a mother or dad. It's fun to imagine what you'll be like some day.

This activity is called "The Story of My Life." It will give you a chance to pretend it's the future ... the near future when you'll have more control over your worries and nervousness. It's like a preview of a movie that's coming soon. This will give you a chance to think a little about what your life will be like when you learn not to fret.

Once you can imagine how it will be, it may make you even more fired up about working to make it happen ... soon!

Simply fill in the blanks and tell your story!

Hi! My name is _____. I want to share with you
the story of my life. I'm mostly a pretty average kid. I am in the _____ grade
at _____ School. I make mostly _____ grades at
school, and my favorite subject is _____. My least favorite subject
is _____. My best friends are _____
and _____.

My family is pretty cool. I live with _____, _____,
_____, _____, _____,
_____. We've lived here for _____ years. I used to live
_____ (name place) before here. (Cross this out if
you haven't lived anywhere else).

One thing pretty special about me is that I love _____
(name your best activity, such as a sport, musical instrument, hobby, or something like
that). My best moment at this was when I _____
_____
(tell about a time you did really well at this activity).

One thing that hasn't been so much fun, though, is that I get kind of nervous a lot. My
biggest worries are _____, _____,
and _____. I guess I first started worrying about stuff
about _____ (years or months) ago. When I get worried, I sometimes
feel nervous feelings like _____, _____,
and _____ (name a couple of the feelings you have in your
body when you feel worried or nervous). My parents and I decided I didn't have to
keep these worries forever, so we started working with _____
(name of your counselor).

My counselor helped me understand more about my worries, and we learned when I worry and what I worry about the most. I also learned about the feelings that go with my worry. My counselor told me to hang in there, and we'd beat these things. Well, she/he was right! My counselor taught me how to relax when I feel stress. She/he also helped me know the ways I think that make me worry. I learned how to change my thinking so I can stop the worries when they show up. Since I learned that, I don't worry nearly so much, and those uncomfortable feelings are gone.

I always had a good life, but now it's even better! Since I learned to beat my worries, I've noticed that I feel _____ (imagine a way you'll feel better when your worries are gone). I also have more time to

_____ (name something fun you can do with the extra time you don't spend worrying). That makes me feel _____!
Not worrying makes school go better because now I don't _____
(think of a change in school when you stop worrying). At home, now I can

_____ (name something you can do when you learn not to worry … like sleep in your own bed, go upstairs without being afraid, etc.).

Best of all, whenever I feel a worry coming on, I remember what I've learned and I say to myself, "I bet I won't fret." It took some work to beat the worries, but I'm really glad I did! I love it now that I don't worry so much!

Take Note

What was the hardest part of writing the story of your life?

_____

_____

_____

_____

What made this kind of hard for you?

_____

_____

_____

_____

What was one thing you learned from this activity?

_____

_____

_____

_____

Write one thing that most excites you as you imagine life without your worries.

_____

_____

_____

_____

Try to think about that thing one time every day as a way of encouraging yourself as you finish your course in beating your worries.

Activity 15   Good Things, Bad Things

> **Assignment:** Learn to notice more of the good
> things that happen every day.

Every day good things happen. Every day bad things happen. But sometimes it seems like we think more about the bad things than the good things. And the more bad things we think about, the more things worry us.

If we notice more good things, it helps us feel better. And it may help us see that there are not as many things to worry about as we thought.

Each night for one week, write down some things that happened that day. Think of four good things and two bad things for each day. You may be surprised at how many good things happen!

You might want to make a copy of the next page so you can do this for more than one week!

Good Things, Bad Things

Activity 15

Good Things

Bad Things

Day 1 1. _____

2. _____

3. _____

4. _____

1. _____

2. _____

Day 2 1. _____

2. _____

3. _____

4. _____

1. _____

2. _____

Day 3 1. _____

2. _____

3. _____

4. _____

1. _____

2. _____

Day 4 1. _____

2. _____

3. _____

4. _____

1. _____

2. _____

Good Things, Bad Things

Day 5   1. _____   1. _____

      2. _____   2. _____

      3. _____

      4. _____

Day 6   1. _____   1. _____

      2. _____   2. _____

      3. _____

      4. _____

Day 7   1. _____   1. _____

      2. _____   2. _____

      3. _____

      4. _____

Take Note

What were three of your favorite good things that happened this week?

_____

_____

_____

Was it easy or hard to think of good things?

_____

_____

_____

How about the bad things? Was it easy or hard to think of them?

_____

_____

_____

Name one thing that helped you think of good things.

_____

_____

_____

Activity 16   Talking to Myself

> ***Assignment:*** Learn to recognize self-talk.

You may not have noticed, but pretty much everybody talks to themselves all of the time. Some people call this "self-talk." Usually this goes on in your mind without your having to think about it. Many of the things you think go by so quickly that you may not even notice them. For example, you know how to get from your room to the kitchen at your house without even thinking about it. This kind of automatic thinking can happen with nervous thoughts, too. If we have some bad habits in our thinking, we may not even notice.

The better you get at noticing your own self-talk, the better you will be at catching worries and nervous thoughts before they get comfortable in your head.

In this activity, you will meet a few kids who are learning to notice their self-talk, too. One of them should be pretty close to your age.

Let's find out what they've learned about talking to themselves!

Recognizing Self-Talk

Note: You may want to get an adult to help you with reading this activity.

Six-year-old Sally Worries About School

Hi! I'm Sally and I'm in kindergarten at Lincoln Elementary. I like to watch TV and play soccer. I like my teacher and my friends at school, but sometimes I feel like crying when I get on the bus in the morning. I didn't really know why until I talked to my dad. He told me that a lot of kids get a little upset when they first start riding the bus to school. He asked me some questions to figure out what was upsetting me. He finally asked me if I was afraid I'd get sick at school, and that was it! He told me my teacher had Mommy's phone number and his, so she could call them if I got sick at school. Wow, did I feel better then!

What did Sally think might happen to her at school?

_____

Now she thinks:

_____

What can she do to solve her problem?

_____

Eight-year-old Andre Worries About Burglars

My name is Andre, and I'm in the second grade. I love to play video games and ride my bike. I've been having a hard time going to sleep at night because I think that someone might break into my house while I'm asleep. I talked to Mom about it, and she said I was safe, but I still worried. I finally talked to a counselor, and she was really neat. She helped me see that I was worrying about something that was pretty much impossible.

She taught me that I was saying what if _____
_____, and then I would think about how burglars could get in.

Now, I say _____ and
think about something else that doesn't worry me, like _____.

Twelve-year-old Latonya Worries About Friends

Hey there! I'm Latonya and I'm in middle school for the first time this year. Wow, are there a lot of kids at my school! My family just moved to this area, so I don't know many of these kids. I'm really shy at school, though I was popular at my old school. I guess I don't want other kids to reject me if they see what I'm really like. Trouble is, I don't talk to anybody much, and that's no way to make friends either. My school counselor thinks I'm saying some things to myself that make me afraid. I think I might be saying things like:

" _____ " or

" _____ ."

But I know these are not really true. So now when I catch myself thinking these things, I stop myself and say instead,

" _____ " or

" _____ ."

Then I feel freer to be my silly and fun-loving self with the other kids.

Fifteen-year-old Walter Worries About His Grades

I'm Walter and I'm a sophomore at Midtown High. I've always made good grades and really want to get a scholarship for college because I know my family can't afford to send me to college without one. I'm having trouble with algebra and I'm scared I'm going to get a D or an F and mess up my college chances forever. I know it's not that bad, but I don't know what to do about it. Got any ideas?

Walter is probably saying something to himself like, *What if* _____

_____; then he'll not get a scholarship and

_____.

Is this really true? _____ What are some other positive things that could happen even if he made an F?

_____

_____

What would you tell him to say instead that might help? _____

_____

Take Note

Why would that help? _____

We'll be doing some activities to learn more about how to recognize, and then change, our self-talk. Some kids will catch on more quickly than others, but you'll get it!

Just for a brief practice, write below what you're saying to yourself about this activity as you finish it:

_____

_____

_____

_____

_____

_____

_____

_____

_____

_____

_____

Activity 17   Self-Talk Researcher

> ***Assignment:*** Learn how people you
> know talk to themselves.

As we work on understanding this self-talk stuff better, it will help to learn from other people. Your job here is to be a research scientist and get information on how other people are using self-talk.

Choose three different people if you can (or use the same person more than once if you can't), and ask them the research survey questions on the activity sheet. You can choose parents, brothers, sisters, friends, grandparents, or even teachers. If you choose a child, it may be better to choose someone a little older than you who may have more experience in noticing his or her self-talk.

Happy researching!

Self-Talk Researcher

Activity 17

#1. Person interviewed: _____

What was that person doing when you talked to them?

_____

_____

Questions to ask:

What are you thinking about right now?

_____

_____

How does thinking about that make you feel?

_____

_____

What does that thought make you want to do?

_____

_____

What does that thought tell you about yourself?

_____

_____

#2. Person interviewed: _____

What was that person doing when you talked to them?

_____

_____

Questions to ask:

What are you thinking about right now?

_____

_____

How does thinking about that make you feel?

_____

_____

What does that thought make you want to do?

_____

_____

What does that thought tell you about yourself?

_____

_____

#3.   Person interviewed: _____

What was that person doing when you talked to them?

_____

_____

Questions to ask:

What are you thinking about right now?

_____

_____

How does thinking about that make you feel?

_____

_____

What does that thought make you want to do?

_____

_____

What does that thought tell you about yourself?

_____

_____

Take Note

Who had the easiest time thinking about his or her self-talk?

_____

_____

_____

_____

Who had the hardest time thinking about his or her self-talk?

_____

_____

_____

_____

Name one thing you noticed in doing your research that might help you with your self-talk.

_____

_____

_____

_____

Name some differences about the way that people talk to themselves.

_____

_____

_____

_____

I Bet I Won't Fret

> ***Assignment:*** Use what you've learned about self-talk to explore your own self-talk.

Now that you've gotten a better idea of self-talk, we're going to try some experiments to see how you talk to yourself in different situations.

You'll also start learning how your self-talk affects the way you think about the future.

Try the three experiments in this activity. Answer the questions before you do the actions for each activity. Then, do the activity and answer the second set of questions.

You're becoming quite a scientist about how people think. Way to go!

Experiment Number 1: Shooting Hoops

In this experiment, you are to shoot a basketball at a basket. This can be a real basketball, with indoor hoop, or even shooting a wadded up piece of paper at a garbage can. Okay, got the ball in your hands and ready to shoot? Great! Before you do, answer these questions:

What am I thinking about myself (like, "I can do it" or "I'm a lousy basketball player," etc.)?

_____

How do I feel as I get ready to shoot? _____

What do I think will happen when I shoot? _____

How will I feel if I make the shot? _____

How will I feel if I miss the shot? _____

What will it say about me if I make the shot? _____

_____

What will it say about me if I miss the shot? _____

_____

NOW ... take the shot! Answer these questions:

Did I make it or miss it? _____

How do I feel about what happened? _____

_____

Finish this statement:

The result of my shot tells me that I am _____.

Experiment Number 2: Asking Permission

This time, your job is to ask someone for permission to do something. You might ask a parent if you may stay up 30 minutes later or ask your sister if you may borrow her CD player or ask a friend if you may borrow a toy. You figure out whom to ask and what you are going to ask. Ready? Now, just before you ask, answer these questions:

What am I thinking about myself (like, "I can do this" or "I'm going to get turned down" or "She won't let me because she doesn't really like me," etc.)?

_____

How do I feel as I get ready to ask? _____

What do I think will happen when I ask? _____

How will I feel if I get permission? _____

How will I feel if I don't get permission? _____

What will it say about me if I get permission? _____

_____

What will it say about me if I get turned down? _____

_____

NOW … ask permission! Answer these questions:

Did I get it or not? _____

How do I feel about what happened? _____

_____

Finish this statement:

The result of asking permission tells me that I am _____.

Experiment Number 3: A Step in the Dark

For some kids, this experiment will be easier than for others. For this experiment, you are simply to step out of your house onto a porch or patio or into the yard while it is dark outside and with no lights on (except those from neighbors' houses and streetlights). All you do is step out, close the door behind you without locking it, and stay for one minute. Then go on back inside. If this is too scary for you, you can have a parent wait at the door or even just skip this activity. Okay, it's dark out and you're ready to go. Answer the following questions:

What am I thinking about myself (like, "I can do this with no problem" or "Are you kidding? This is TOO scary for me" or "I'm not too sure if I can do this or not," etc.)?

_____

How do I feel as I get ready to step outside? _____

What do I think will happen when I step outside? _____

How will I feel when I step outside? _____

How will I feel if I decide I can't do it? _____

What will it say about me if I make it? _____

_____

What will it say about me if I decide I can't do it? _____

_____

NOW … step outside in the dark for one minute! Answer these questions:

Did I make it or decide not to do it? ._____

Take Note

This activity was a little work, wasn't it? Way to hang in there and get it done!

There are at least three things you can learn from this:

1. Notice what you are thinking when you are doing something or even before you do it.

2. Think about what to expect or what will happen after you do something. (Usually we have some ideas before we do it of what we think will happen.)

3. Think about how you feel after you do something.

In your case, did what you expected to do or feel happen or not?

_____

_____

_____

_____

What surprises did you have in how you did or how you felt after the experiments?

_____

_____

_____

_____

Outstanding! You're getting the hang of self-talk.

Activity 19

Knowing My Nervous Self-Talk

> ***Assignment:*** Learn about how you talk to yourself when you're nervous or worried.

You now know quite a bit about self-talk. It's time to use it to get a better grip on your nervous and worried thinking.

In this activity, keep track of 10 times you catch yourself worrying. (You might also ask a parent or someone else to mention to you when they see you worrying.) Using the self-talk chart in this exercise, think about your self-talk during those times. This activity may be done in one day or it may take a few days. The main thing is to learn more about what you say to yourself that makes you worried or nervous.

Knowing My Nervous Self-Talk

What I Was Worried About	What I Said to Myself About That Thing	The Bad Thing I Thought Might Happen	How I Felt About This
Example: My math test	What if I don't pass it?	I'll fail and get in big trouble	Really worried
#1			
#2			
#3			
#4			
#5			
#6			
#7			
#8			
#9			
#10			

Take Note

Well, that was interesting! As you kept a record of your self-talk, you may have noticed some patterns. Many … and maybe most … worries come from what are called expectations. They are things that you figure are going to happen in the future. If you expect bad things to happen, you may worry. If you expect good things to happen, you get excited.

List three of the bad things you learned that you expect to happen when you are worrying:

#1_____

#2_____

#3_____

Now, here's a curious question. When you think about each of these things while you're not worried, what do you think really might happen? In the example about the math test, the child's parents might have been disappointed if she did poorly on the test, but probably they wouldn't be super mad, and she wouldn't fail the grade over just one test.

Try to think differently about your three expectations, and write your answers below. As always, if this is a little tricky for you, ask a parent or someone else to help.

When I think about the three bad things without worrying, my expectations are:

#1_____

#2_____

#3_____

We'll learn more later, but for now, notice that one of the secrets to beating worry is to change your expectations about what will happen.

Assignment: Put together a
plan to beat your worries!

You've learned a lot so far. You've learned how worries work, how they make you feel, and how your thinking can help or hurt the situation. Now that you understand how worries work, we will focus on how to battle them.

For this assignment, you simply fill out the plan on the activity sheet. Your parents or counselor may help you with this. Fill in as much as you can for now. Fill in more as you learn new strategies for fighting fretting. Use what you have learned to fill these in, including *Things I Worry About* (pages 13 and 14), *How Anxious Am I? Nervous Thermometer* (page 21), *My Nervous Mountain* (pages 37 and 38), and *Anxiety Ladder* (pages 40 and 41).

Name: _____ **Date** _____

The first worry I want to beat is _____.

When I worry about this, I feel (list emotions and feelings you have in your body, too):

_____

When I worry about this, I say to myself: _____

_____.

Then I expect this to happen: _____.

The times I worry about this the most are _____,

_____, and _____.

My Plan

To beat my nervous feelings, I will (choose activities you learned and say how you will use them against this particular worry):

_____

_____

_____

_____

To beat my nervous thoughts, I will (choose activities you learned and say how you will use them against this particular worry):

_____

_____

_____

_____

Name: _____ **Date** _____

The second worry I want to beat is _____.

When I worry about this, I feel (list emotions and feelings you have in your body, too):

_____

When I worry about this, I say to myself: _____

_____.

Then I expect this to happen: _____.

The times I worry about this the most are _____,

_____, and _____.

My Plan

To beat my nervous feelings, I will (choose activities you learned and say how you will use them against this particular worry):

_____

_____

_____

_____

To beat my nervous thoughts, I will (choose activities you learned and say how you will use them against this particular worry):

_____

_____

_____

_____

Name: _____ **Date** _____

The third worry I want to beat is _____.

When I worry about this, I feel (list emotions and feelings you have in your body, too):

_____

When I worry about this, I say to myself: _____

_____.

Then I expect this to happen: _____.

The times I worry about this the most are _____,

_____, and _____.

My Plan

To beat my nervous feelings, I will (choose activities you learned and say how you will use them against this particular worry):

_____

_____

_____

_____

To beat my nervous thoughts, I will (choose activities you learned and say how you will use them against this particular worry):

_____

_____

_____

_____

Take Note

Did you write a good plan? Feel free to change it if you need to and add to it as you learn new things.

Having an anti-anxious plan is a great step to victory over nervous thoughts and feelings.

Write an idea to help you remember to look at this plan every day to remind you what you are working on:

_____

_____

_____

_____

_____

_____

_____

_____

_____

_____

Good luck!

Activity 21   Breathe Deeply!

> ### *Assignment:* Learn how to use breathing to feel less nervous.

In this and the next two activities, you are going to work on relaxing your body when you worry.

It's kind of funny—when we worry, our body reacts by getting excited and ready to act. That's great when you have something to really be worried about.

Say a giant grizzly bear walks into your house one day. I'd suggest you worry at that point. Your body will get excited, and that helps you to run faster to get away from the bear. But it isn't very much fun to get excited like that if there isn't anything to run from. And if your body gets worked up like that, you may feel scared even though there's nothing to be scared of. In fact, many times when you are nervous, you breathe faster automatically, even though breathing slower is better for you. So, we're going to learn how to calm our bodies down when we are feeling nervous for no good reason.

One of the easiest ways to calm down is to breathe differently. In this activity, you will learn how to change your breathing. This will be really handy when you're nervous or worried.

In this activity, you might ask a parent, brother, sister, or someone else to read the directions for you so you can pay better attention to breathing. Try the exercise five times over the next few days.

It's time to learn to control your breathing better. Sit down in a comfortable chair with a back and arms. Sit pretty straight and rest your arms on the arms of the chair. If this isn't comfortable for you, find a position for your arms that is.

Close your eyes and pay attention to your breathing. Notice the rising and falling of your chest as you breathe in and out several times. Enjoy the relaxed feeling that comes as you breathe out. It seems like your body is sinking deeper into the chair as you do.

Now take a deep breath; then see how slowly you can let it out. This will make you feel more and more relaxed as you do it. Do this three times. Take a deep breath, and then very slowly let it out.

Great. This time, when you have let all the air out at the end of your breath, count to five slowly: one … two … three … four … five. Now breathe in deeply and let your air out slowly. Count to five again and repeat this four more times.

As you do this, notice how relaxed you start to feel. You might even feel a little sleepy. What is cool about this is that you calmed down all by yourself … just by slowing down and breathing carefully.

Good job. Now breathe normally a couple of times and you're ready to get up and get back to what you were doing … only you're feeling a bit more relaxed as you do it!

Take Note

Now you know how to relax yourself by breathing deeply and slowly.

Briefly describe the feelings you had while you did this activity:

_____

_____

_____

_____

Now you are ready to use this when you worry or feel nervous. You may not have time to sit down and go through the whole exercise, but you can take a few deep breaths the next time you are fretting or nervous. Practice this as much as you can. Maybe you can ask your parents or teacher to remind you to breathe deeply when they notice that you seem nervous or worried.

Great! You're starting to beat your anxiety. Your hard work is really paying off!

> ***Assignment:*** Choose a favorite place that is really peaceful to you.

The deep breathing felt pretty good, didn't it? Now you're going to make it even better by learning to relax your whole body. Being nervous or worried is NOT relaxing, but you can make yourself relaxed when you wish. It just takes a little practice.

Before we learn to relax even better, I want you to think of a place that is really peaceful and relaxing for you. It might be lying on the beach or relaxing by a campfire in the mountains or quietly resting in a religious setting or sitting in your backyard looking at the stars. Wherever it is, choose your most peaceful place. Think about it a few minutes and get as many details in your mind as you can. Now you're ready to describe your place on the activity sheet.

Just a reminder: choose a place that's really calm and relaxing, not an exciting kind of place. An amusement park or video arcade may be one of your favorite places, but they are not relaxing places. Think of a place that helps you feel calm and relaxed.

For my peaceful place, I chose:

_____

The main reason this is my most peaceful place is that:

_____

_____

Describe what you see when you are there:

_____

_____

Describe what you hear when you are there:

_____

_____

Describe what you smell when you are there:

_____

_____

Describe what you feel when you are there:

_____

_____

Now draw a picture of this place on the next page.

A Picture of My Most Peaceful Place

Take Note

It's fun to think about peaceful places. It's surprising how much noise and activity are around us most of the time. That can be exciting, but sometimes we need to get away and be quiet and relaxed.

What would your second choice of peaceful place be?

_____

Think of three times when you'd like to be at your peaceful place:

#1 _____

#2 _____

#3 _____

Why might a peaceful place be helpful when you are fretting or nervous?

_____

_____

Even if you can't go to your peaceful place every time you're feeling bad, thinking about it will be a big help to your worries. This will be even better when you learn a little more about relaxing.

I Bet I Won't Fret

> ***Assignment:*** Learn to relax yourself.

Your peaceful place sounds pretty cool. Now you'll learn how to relax your muscles while thinking about that place.

For this activity, it is better if you have someone read the instructions to you so you can focus on your peaceful place and follow the instructions. It will teach you how to relax your whole body … and it's neat to know that you can do this yourself. Even when your body feels nervous, you can take charge and calm it down with exercises like these. That's another way to beat nervous feelings and worries. You don't have to do what the worries say or to feel helpless about being upset. You can take charge of how relaxed you are … and that feels GOOD!

Practice this relaxation exercise at least three times over the next few days. You might even want to teach another member of your family how to do this. Everybody enjoys being relaxed when they are stressed!

Take a seat just as you did in the deep-breathing exercise. Go through a few deep breaths as we practiced there. As you get comfortable, imagine you are at your most relaxing place. Picture yourself there. Imagine the sounds you would hear and the feelings you would have. Even try to imagine the smells you would smell. Enjoy the calm feelings you have.

Now let's try to get even more relaxed. Start with your lower body. Tighten the muscles in your legs and feet and hold them tight for a few seconds. Can you feel the tension? Now, slowly relax your leg and foot muscles and enjoy the good feeling you have as these muscles ease up. Is it all comfortable, or do you notice any parts that don't feel very relaxed? Try to relax any areas that still feel tense.

Now pay attention to the middle of your body. Notice the relaxation of your muscles when you breathe out and the tension when you take a breath. Tighten the muscles in your bottom and hold them tight for a few seconds. Now, slowly release the tension and feel pleasant feelings as the muscles relax. Next tighten your tummy muscles for a few seconds and then relax them. Notice how your heartbeat is slowing and how peaceful you feel. Pause just a second to think again about your peaceful place and keep pretending you are there.

Now pay attention to your arms. Tighten your arms and clench your fists. Hold this tension for a few seconds and notice the tightness. Okay, now slowly, slowly relax these muscles and pay attention to the good sensation. Feels pretty good, huh?

Now pay attention to your head and neck. Squint your eyes really hard and tighten your neck muscles. Hold this for a few seconds and slowly relax these muscles. Now smile a really big smile to tighten the muscles in your face. Feel the tension in these muscles for a few seconds and relax them slowly.

Relax! Activity 23

Take a moment to enjoy the good feeling of relaxation all over your body. Picture in your mind your peaceful place again. Check to make sure you are still breathing slowly and deeply. Remember this good feeling—a good, calm feeling that you made by learning to relax. Think of how much better this feels than stress and nervousness. And remember you can choose to change nervous feelings to relaxed ones if you wish!

Now, slowly lift your arms and open your eyes. You might stretch for just a minute and open your eyes to remind yourself you're still in your chair. You are now ready to get up and face the rest of your day, feeling relaxed and ready.

Take Note

Excellent—you are really getting the hang of calming yourself. Doesn't it feel good to be able to control our bodies and not feel trapped by anxious feelings and thoughts? Take just a minute to think about this.

What surprised you when you practiced relaxing?

_____

_____

_____

How does it feel to know you can control your body and relax it whenever you choose?

_____

_____

_____

How do you think this will be useful in beating your worries and nervous feelings?

_____

_____

_____

Riding the Wave

> **Assignment:** Learn to understand and ride "waves" of nervous feelings.

Okay, now we're getting ready to use our new relaxation tools in the battle against our fretting. Sometimes nervous feelings come on us when we're worrying. Sometimes they start up all by themselves. Either way, the secret is to pay attention to them so you can handle them before they handle you!

Kids often have a time when nervous feelings come on them, then get worse, and sometimes get really scary. The tricky part is that if these feelings upset you, they'll get even worse. It's like giving a hungry tiger a little bite to eat; it then only wants more! So, beating the feelings that come with being nervous will mean you notice the feelings early and don't let them get to you.

In this activity, you are to catch your nervous "wave" a few times, then beat it by "riding" it and fighting it with deep breathing and relaxation.

Fill in the blanks to get a good understanding of your "waves" of anxiety and then keep a record of a few times you manage to ride those waves. Think of the deep breathing as your "boogie board" at the beach. Have fun!

We have learned that when you start to get nervous, you have the following feelings:

_____, _____, and _____, but

the first way you can tell you are getting anxious is that you start to feel

_____. These feelings can get scary, and the more they scare you,

the more they grow.

So, we know that these feelings won't hurt you, and if you don't let them scare you, they'll go away, like a wave in the ocean.

Imagine yourself standing in the ocean and a smooth, not-too-big wave is coming. You feel the water gently lift you up but you know that the wave will soon pass on by. And it does, setting you down as gently as it lifted you. Knowing how waves work helped you through what could have been a scary situation. It was actually a lot of fun!

This is how anxious feelings work. When you feel _____ (the first sensation of the sense of panic) coming, you say, "Hey! I know what this is! It's just a nervous feeling. If I don't fight it, like a wave, it'll pass. Yep, here it comes. I know you, feeling. You're just rolling by and you'll be gone in just a minute. I feel you a bit more now, so the wave is under me. I feel a worry coming on, but nothing bad is going to happen. I'm just reacting to the feeling and I don't have to worry. This is probably a good time to work on my deep breathing. And I'll try to get in a more relaxed position and try to relax any muscles I notice are tense."

I Bet I Won't Fret

It's kind of fun knowing how these feelings work. Ah, there it goes, leaving you. The feeling wave is headed toward shore and will crash there. That was cool! You handled it and didn't let the nervous thoughts make the feelings worse. You're going to beat this nervous stuff!

Record of riding the waves:

Day	Time	Where Was I?		How Did It Go? (circle one)		
			Great	Good	Okay	Not good
			Great	Good	Okay	Not good
			Great	Good	Okay	Not good
			Great	Good	Okay	Not good
			Great	Good	Okay	Not good
			Great	Good	Okay	Not good
			Great	Good	Okay	Not good
			Great	Good	Okay	Not good
			Great	Good	Okay	Not good
			Great	Good	Okay	Not good

Take Note

Well, how did it go? How was your wave riding?

What things seemed to be really helpful to you in beating the waves of nervous feelings?

_____

_____

_____

_____

What things did you have trouble with when the nervous feelings got to be pretty strong?

_____

_____

_____

_____

What can you work on that will help you be a better wave rider?

_____

_____

_____

_____

> ***Assignment:*** Learn how to solve problems well and practice doing this.

Life is full of problems. But problems usually don't have to be problems. They can be opportunities. If you play a tennis game against a really good player, it may be a problem to win but it's a great opportunity to get better at tennis. A tough spelling test may be a problem, but it's an opportunity to show what you can do when you really study.

Sometimes, problems worry us because we don't know how to solve them or we're nervous that our solutions won't be very good. So, the better we are at problem solving, the less we'll worry. The more confident we feel in our problem-solving skills, the less we'll be nervous about our problems.

In this assignment, you'll learn the five steps to problem solving. Go over these with a parent or friend. The better you know these, the better you'll be able to use them. Then you will be better at figuring out your worries.

Then, try your skills with the examples given. You'll be a master of problem solving when you work out a problem of your own at the end.

Let's get started!

Five Steps to Solving Problems

Step 1. Clearly define the problem.

Example 1:

I don't get my homework finished in time to see my favorite show at 7:30.

Example 2:

I get nervous every time my mom goes to the store and leaves me home with my big sister.

Step 2. Think up at least four different solutions to the problem.

Example 1:

Give up on watching my TV show.

Do my homework so fast that I don't do a good job. Do my homework before I come home from school.

Do my homework as soon as I get home from school.

Example 2:

Make Mom take me with her every time. Beg Mom not to go to the store.

Stay right beside my sister the whole time Mom is gone. Figure out a way to beat the nervous feelings.

Step 3. Evaluate the different solutions. (Think of how they'll work out right now and in the long run.)

Example 1:

That would get my homework done, but I hate the thought of not getting to see my favorite TV show anymore.

This way I would get to see my show, and that would be fun; but Dad will be unhappy if I do crummy on my homework, and I'd end up making bad grades.

If I do my homework before I come home from school, wow, I'd be free all afternoon and evening. No problem seeing my show then, and I don't get into trouble about my schoolwork. But this won't work every day because I don't always have enough time to do my homework before I leave school. So, I would either not get my homework done some days or still have to miss my TV show.

This would mean I couldn't goof off for an hour after school like I enjoy; but if I went ahead and got my homework done, it would feel good to be free from school, and I wouldn't have to miss my TV show.

Example 2:

If I went with Mom every time, I wouldn't get nervous. But I don't really like walking through the grocery store, and this would probably slow Mom down, too.

I would like it if Mom didn't have to go, but let's get real here. If she doesn't go to the store, we don't have groceries and stuff. Besides, I don't think she would let me get away with making her stay home all the time.

I'm less nervous when I'm right with my sister, but that's no fun at all. She talks on the phone and stuff, and that would bore me and make her grouchy, all at the same time.

I'm not sure about how to beat the nervous feelings, but if I think about it really hard, I know Mom will be okay. After all, my sister isn't worried about Mom. I'll feel more grown up if I learn not to be nervous, too. I'll try my deep breathing and tell myself Mom will be okay. Then I'll get busy so I don't think about it so much.

Step 4. Put the best solution into action.

Example 1:

Okay, then tomorrow I'll plan to do my homework as soon as I get home from school and then I'll be finished before my TV show.

Example 2:

When Mom goes to the store today, I won't whine or complain, and I won't ask to go with her. I'll tell myself this isn't a good worry because Mom can take care of herself, and I'll be okay at home with my sister. If I feel nervous, I'll ride my wave and do my breathing and relaxation.

Step 5. Reward yourself for trying a new solution that worked. (If it didn't work, go back to Step 2 and think of more choices and then move ahead from there.)

Example 1:

Hot dog! I've seen my show every night for a week. I think I'll celebrate by making popcorn to eat during the show tonight!

Example 2:

Well, that wasn't so bad. I got a little nervous when Mom went to the store today, but I thought about my worries and didn't give in to them. I relaxed and made it through. I bet it gets easier from here! Next time, I'll reward myself by calling my best friend while Mom is gone.

Now try these on your own.

Problem #1: Sally can't decide which of her four best friends to invite over to spend the night.

Step 1: _____

Step 2:

    Idea #1 _____

    Idea #2 _____

    Idea #3 _____

    Idea #4 _____

Step 3:

    Idea #1 _____

    _____

    Idea #2 _____

    _____

    Idea #3 _____

    _____

    Idea #4 _____

    _____

Step 4:

Winning idea # _____

How did you do? (You'll have to make this up, but pretend it worked out great.)

_____

Step 5: Reward: _____

Problem #2: Martin worries about robbers when he goes to bed and can't go to sleep without having one of his parents sit in his room.

Step 1: _____

Step 2:

Idea #1 _____

Idea #2 _____

Idea #3 _____

Idea #4 _____

Step 3:

Idea #1 _____

_____

Idea #2 _____

_____

Idea #3 _____

_____

Idea #4 _____

_____

Step 4:

Winning idea # _____

How did you do? (You'll have to make this up, but pretend it worked out great.)

_____

Step 5: Reward: _____

Problem #3: Now work on a problem of your own.

Step 1: _____

Step 2:

    Idea #1 _____

    Idea #2 _____

    Idea #3 _____

    Idea #4 _____

Step 3:

    Idea #1 _____

    _____

    Idea #2 _____

    _____

    Idea #3 _____

    _____

    Idea #4 _____

    _____

Step 4:

Winning idea # _____

How did you do? (You'll have to make this up, but pretend it worked out great.)

_____

Step 5: Reward: _____

Take Note

That was very good work. That was a tough exercise, but now you've learned something that should be really helpful in beating your worries.

Before we move on, try one brief activity here: write down three more problems in your life that you could solve with your new skills.

Problem #1

_____

_____

Problem #2

_____

_____

Problem #3

_____

_____

I Bet I Won't Fret

Stop That Thought!   Activity 26

> ***Assignment:*** Learn to stop nervous thoughts.

You know by now that nervous feelings have much to do with nervous thinking. Kids who are nervous simply worry about more things than other kids. But what makes this a big problem is that most kids worry almost without even noticing it.

So, the first thing to do for beating the worries is to learn to catch yourself when you are thinking nervous thoughts and stop them. Once you get pretty good at stopping them, you'll learn how to get rid of them better in the next few activities.

For now, I just want you to work on catching yourself when you are worrying. You probably know that most of your worries don't help things very much anyway. Besides, worrying isn't exactly a fun thing to do. Have you ever said, "Mom, I'm really bored. Will you tell me something to worry about so I can have a little fun?" I don't think so.

Here's the plan. Whenever you catch yourself worrying about things you don't need to, say to yourself, "Stop that!" You aren't a slave to your thinking, and you can take charge of it! The worry may want to argue with you, but you can be tough and argue back, "I don't have to worry if I don't want to." Even if you lose some of these arguments and keep worrying, at least you know you're catching the worries and fighting them. That's where you have to start.

On the next pages, keep a record of the times you remembered to talk back to your worries and told them to stop. Then note what you were worrying about and how you did in arguing with your worries.

Go get 'em!

Activity 26

Stop That Thought!

Day/Time	What Was I Worrying About?	How Did I Do Trying to Stop It?		
		Great	Okay	Not so good
		Great	Okay	Not so good
		Great	Okay	Not so good
		Great	Okay	Not so good
		Great	Okay	Not so good
		Great	Okay	Not so good
		Great	Okay	Not so good
		Great	Okay	Not so good
		Great	Okay	Not so good
		Great	Okay	Not so good
		Great	Okay	Not so good
		Great	Okay	Not so good

I Bet I Won't Fret

Take Note

I hope you had some good practice stopping your worries. How did you do?

_____

_____

_____

Did you notice that you started to get better at catching your worries?

_____

_____

_____

Did you get better as you practiced?

_____

_____

_____

Share one secret you figured out that seemed to help you.

_____

_____

_____

WELL DONE!

Activity 27

Worry Time

> ### *Assignment:* Learn to control when you worry about stuff.

You may have noticed that just saying "Stop it!" to your worries did not stop them. They're pretty stubborn thoughts, those worries! Our next step is a plan that lets you still worry about these things if you need to, but helps keep them from bothering you when you're busy doing something else.

This activity is actually pretty easy. Decide on a time for each day when you are free to worry about stuff. Mark it on your Worry-Time sheet. Then, during the day, write down any worry that comes to your mind so you can worry about it at the time you decided. This means that you can still worry, but only at a certain time. Not only does this slow down your worries during the day, but it also helps you take more control of the worries instead of their being so bossy. You might also find that when you get to worry time, the worries aren't as big as you might have thought.

Write down things that come to mind during the day so you can worry about them later instead.

Sunday. My Worry Time today will be at _____ o'clock.
Things to worry about:

1. _____

2. _____

3. _____

4. _____

5. _____

Monday. My Worry Time today will be at _____ o'clock.
Things to worry about:

1. _____

2. _____

3. _____

4. _____

5. _____

Tuesday. My Worry Time today will be at _____ o'clock.
Things to worry about:

1. _____

2. _____

3. _____

4. _____

5. _____

Wednesday. My Worry Time today will be at _____ o'clock.
Things to worry about:

1. _____

2. _____

3. _____

4. _____

5. _____

Thursday. My Worry Time today will be at _____ o'clock.
Things to worry about:

1. _____

2. _____

3. _____

4. _____

5. _____

Friday. My Worry Time today will be at _____ o'clock.
Things to worry about:

1. _____

2. _____

3. _____

4. _____

5. _____

Saturday. My Worry Time today will be at _____ o'clock.
Things to worry about:

1. _____

2. _____

3. _____

4. _____

5. _____

> ***Assignment:*** Learn to figure out which worries are real and which are mostly not real.

Most worries are tough because most have at least a really small chance of coming to pass. I have often told kids in my office that I can't promise them that a meteor won't come streaking through my window and land on the floor between us. Kids agree that this is probably a pretty silly thing to worry about. They agree that I would not be wise to stop doing my job to stare out the window just in case a meteor happens to be coming. The odds are a gazillion to one against it, but it IS possible.

On the other hand, if you are hiking in the woods and hear the sound of a rattlesnake shaking its tail at you to warn you, then you can be pretty sure you need to worry and take immediate action.

The tough part is that most worries are not that easy to figure out. If you are worried about a burglar breaking into your house, no one can really promise that that will never happen. Your mom or dad may tell you that most burglars know better than to come at night when people are home or that you have a really good alarm system or that home burglars are really rare or that even if a burglar came, your parents would hear them and call the police long before they ever got to your room. STILL, there is that teeny tiny chance a burglar could show up. But this is SUCH a small chance, it's not worth the worry.

This activity offers a list of questions you can ask yourself to help decide if this is really something to worry about or not. It will help you think about some of your worries and decide if they are worth the trouble or not. Page 109 includes a couple of worries to practice on. Then try a few of your own.

The worry I'm wondering about is:

_____

Question 1. Is this something that has ever happened to me for real?

_____

_____

_____

Question 2. Is this very likely to happen? Is it more like a meteor showing up, or more like a sure thing?

_____

_____

_____

Question 3. What have other people told me about how real this worry is?

_____

_____

_____

Question 4. What is the worst thing that could happen if this worry came true?

_____

_____

Question 5. Yes, but what is the MOST LIKELY thing to happen if this worry came true? (That is, try to think what would REALLY happen. Don't imagine the worst that could happen.)

_____

_____

Question 6. List several reasons this worry probably won't happen.

_____

_____

_____

Question 7. What can I do to make it even less likely that this worry will happen (for example, lock the door if I'm scared of someone breaking in)?

_____

_____

_____

Question 8. What could I do that would be more useful or fun than worrying about this thing?

_____

_____

_____

SO ... IS THIS WORTH WORRYING ABOUT?

_____ Yes

_____ No

Practice with:

I am worried my dad might be in an automobile accident.

I am worried that I'll never have any friends.

I am worried that I'll get hurt playing baseball.

Try a worry of your own.

Take Note

You may have noticed that most worries are not worth the trouble. This is especially true if you can't do anything to keep the bad thing from happening. The worry doesn't make it less likely to happen, but it does make you miss out on things you'd rather be doing.

Why do you think it's still kind of hard to stop worrying even if you know it's a mostly unreal worry?

_____

_____

_____

_____

What skills have you learned so far in your work that would help you battle your unreal worries?

_____

_____

_____

_____

Remember: Worries can be stubborn, but you can still beat them with some good work!

Activity 29   Order in the Court

> ***Assignment:*** Practice arguing with the idea that terrible things may happen.

It's one thing to worry a lot, but many times, the worry is worse because you get to thinking that terrible things might happen. For example, it's bad enough to wonder why your friend didn't call you back when you left her a message, but this gets really crummy when you start to think that it's because she hates you ... and that's probably because nobody really likes you ... and so you'll never have any friends ever. Suddenly, one phone call has you afraid you'll never have ANY friends.

This is called catastrophic thinking—thinking that things will be a catastrophe. It happens when you take a little worry or problem and make it into something huge, or at least bigger than it ought to be. This is a common problem for people who get nervous a lot.

Most kids know when they do this that they are getting carried away. But it's pretty hard to stop it. In this activity, you will pretend to put catastrophic thinking on trial to see if there is enough evidence to prove things are as bad as you think. In a courtroom, each side presents the facts that support their side of a situation. Then a judge decides which side has the best evidence to prove its point. If you don't really understand how a court works, ask an older person to explain it to you.

Choose a worry that sometimes gets you thinking really scary stuff, and use it for the activity. This should be a fun way to imagine putting your worries "on trial" to see if things are as bad as you may think. If not, then you can say to them, "GUILTY!" on the charge of making you worry too much. Punish those thoughts by sending them away and not listening to them anymore!

We are gathered here today to put your catastrophic thinking on trial. Here's the case: You are worried that what will happen?

_____

And if this happens, you are thinking this terrible thing will follow:

_____

This worry is being charged with making you fret when you don't need to. First, what things make it sound like this terrible thing really will happen? Write all the things you can think of that you believe make it LIKELY that this will happen.

_____

_____

Next, can you think of any time something like this has ever happened to you or to someone?

_____

Now it's time for the other side to try to prove that this isn't such a big deal after all. First, if this never has happened to you or someone you know, why do you think it could happen now?

_____

_____

If you think calmly, is that a good reason? _____

What are some reasons that, even if this bad thing happened, it would not be as bad as you are thinking?

_____

_____

What are some reasons that this bad thing probably won't happen anyway?

_____

_____

Now, you decide. Is this thought true or is it guilty of making you worry more than you need to?

_____

If it is guilty, tell what you will do to keep it from bothering you again:

_____

Excellent. Court is closed.

Take Note

Way to hang in there. That one may have been a little hard for you to understand. Sticking with it is great, and a good skill for handling pesky worries.

Name one thing that you found interesting in this activity:

_____

List three other things that may be catastrophic thoughts that worry you:

1. _____

2. _____

3. _____

Try to think these through to see if you can prove that they are not worth all the worry you're putting into them.

Way to work!

Activity 30   Learning to Argue with My Worries

> **Assignment:** Learn how to argue with your worries so you can beat them.

You're probably starting to feel as if you're getting a little more control of your worries. Worries become a problem when we worry about things that are almost certain never to happen. Or sometimes we worry too much about something that's only worth a little worry. You should be a little concerned about a big test at school, but it's not worth getting sick or losing sleep over. And, of course, any worries about monsters are not really helpful since, except for pretend ones in the movies, there are no real monsters.

When we worry about something more than we should, we have to face it: the worries are kind of like lies. They're not really true, and it's kind of naughty of our brains to say stuff like that to us. We have to learn how to argue with that rude part of our brains that makes us worry about stuff.

In this activity, you are to listen to how some other kids argue with their worries to help you learn how to argue with yours.

There are three steps:

1. Ask: Why would this be an okay thing to worry about?

2. Ask: Why is this a silly worry?

3. Decide: What am I going to think of instead?

Look for these in the stories that follow.

Learning to Argue with My Worries Activity 30

Jose Worries About Thunderstorms

My name is Jose, and I am 11 years old. I was sitting in class the other day, looking out the window. I started worrying, "What if we have a bad thunderstorm?" This got me feeling really nervous, and I even stopped listening to my teacher talking to us. Finally, I remembered to stop that thought. Then I had a little talk with myself. Is it worth worrying about a thunderstorm? I decided it wasn't. Why not? Because even if we had one, our school building is really strong and our teachers will protect us. But it is silly to worry about it anyway. Why? Because every cloud doesn't mean a thunderstorm, and the weather forecast even said it was only supposed to be "partly cloudy" today. So it's almost a sure thing that we won't have a thunderstorm today. And if we did, I already know that I'll be safe. This is a rude worry because it is trying to get my mind off my lessons, and making a bad grade if I don't listen IS something to worry about. So, hush up, rude worry. Back to listening to my teacher....

Why did Jose decide a thunderstorm wasn't worth worrying about, even if one came?

_____

_____

Why did he decide it was silly to worry about a thunderstorm coming anyway?

_____

_____

What did he decide to think about instead?

_____

_____

A Workbook to Help Children with Generalized Anxiety Disorder 119

Nancy Worries About Her Vocabulary Test

I'm Nancy and I'm in fourth grade. This Friday is a big vocabulary test, and I'm really worried about it. What if I went in there and just forgot everything? Last night when I was trying to go to sleep, I kept thinking about the test and if I should get up and study some more. Then I said, "Wait a minute! This isn't a good plan." I thought about whether this was a good thing to worry about. Yeah, of course, I want to do well on my test. I've always made good grades and don't want to mess up now. But then I realized I was way TOO worried. It's really silly, you see. Like I just said, I've always made good grades, so why wouldn't I do it this time? And what's really goofy is I know that if I'm tired, I won't do well. And the more I worry, the less rest I get. What's the worst that could happen? I'd forget a couple of answers. I still have enough good grades to get an A in the class. So, I decided it was more relaxing to think about my pleasant place. I stopped worrying and started thinking about relaxing at my favorite beach. Now THAT helped me get to sleep!

Why did Nancy think it was okay to be a little concerned about her vocabulary test?

_____

_____

But why did Nancy decide it was silly to be worrying about it so much … especially at bedtime?

_____

_____

What did Nancy decide to think about instead?

_____

_____

Li Mae Worries About Getting Sick

My name is Li Mae, and I'm 13 years old. I am very active and enjoy sports. Yesterday I was at a class party at school and got to thinking about all the people there. I heard a boy cough and I got to wondering, "What if I get sick? I won't be able to play in the volleyball game Saturday!" Wow, I felt pretty upset! Then I thought to myself, "Hey, I don't have to fret!" I asked myself, "Will I get sick from being around these other kids?" Not really, I decided. Lots of things can make you sick. I even heard that by getting stressed out you can make it easier to get sick. Besides, what good was it doing me to worry about it? There are germs anywhere I go. So long as I'm careful to wash my hands before I eat, I should be okay. So, I chose not to worry anymore. There is a new girl in class I wanted to meet, so I decided I would walk over and talk to her instead. That was cool! Instead of getting all worked up over nothing, now I have a new friend!

Why did Li Mae decide worrying about getting sick wasn't an okay worry?

_____

_____

Why did Li Mae decide worrying about getting sick was a bit silly?

_____

_____

What did Li Mae think instead?

_____

_____

Take Note

These three children all had to work at it, but they managed to change worries into good things. Because the funny thing is, whenever you are worrying, you're missing a chance to do something that's really better for you. It may be listening in class, relaxing, or even making a new friend.

Think of three things that your worrying has kept you from doing at times:

_____

_____

_____

What would be one thing you could do to help you remember to argue with your worries?

_____

_____

> ### *Assignment:* Learn to handle your worries without bugging other people.

You're learning a whole bunch of skills to fight your worries. But you have to use them for them to work. Here's a problem: when you are worried about something, it may feel easier to just ask a parent, teacher, or friend to reassure you that things will be okay. If you are afraid you are getting sick, though you know you really aren't, it still feels pretty good to ask your mom and have her say, "You're fine." But this—strangely enough—can make your worries grow stronger sometimes because you did not fight them in your head in the way we've been learning.

It is REALLY a challenge not to ask others for reassurance when you are worried, especially after you've been doing it for a while.

It's kind of like this. My dog loves to beg at the table when I'm eating. I sometimes give him food, thinking maybe he'll quit begging. Does he? Of course not. In fact, he only begs more. That's because I'm giving in to the begging and not making my dog learn to deal with it himself. You'll stop worrying more quickly if you get over it yourself, without others giving you reassurance.

Your assignment this time is to argue with your worries rather than get another person to comfort them. This means you have to admit that these aren't really things you need to worry about. Then you need to argue with them and get your mind on something else. Every time you do that, write down your success. This may be pretty tough at first, but it gets easier as you practice. When you get to 10, give yourself a treat!

My list of times I handled my worry without asking someone else to help me:

Number Day   Time   **What I Was Worrying About**

1. _____

2. _____

3. _____

4. _____

5. _____

6. _____

7. _____

8. _____

9. _____

10. _____

Take Note

Very good work! Was it easy or hard to do this?

_____

_____

_____

Did it get easier as you practiced?

_____

_____

_____

What plan did you use that helped you do this activity?

_____

_____

_____

What advice would you give other kids to help them handle their worries alone?

_____

_____

_____

Great! Now just keep practicing this and you'll be able to say, "I bet I won't fret."

Activity 32　　　Yeah, I Can Do THAT!

> **Assignment:** Face a nervous situation that you have been scared of.

When a lot of things make you nervous, it's pretty easy to just try to avoid them. But in our last few exercises, you've been learning to argue with your worries and face them. That's really cool, because a fear faced is a fear beaten. The more you face things that make you nervous, the more confidence you get that you won't fret the next time something scares you.

In this activity, you are to read two stories about other kids who faced nervous situations and won. You are to write down one thing you learned from each.

Next, write a plan for how you will handle a situation that makes you anxious. You might have a parent or counselor help you develop the plan.

Finally, do it! Do the thing that had you scared and win one more battle over anxiety!

Yeah, I Can Do THAT!

Ahmed Rides the Tornado!

Hi, I'm Ahmed and I'm 11 years old. I love to go to amusement parks. We had a class trip to our local park, and I was embarrassed. I was the only one in my group who was scared to ride the Tornado, a roller coaster that goes upside down. They had a fun time on it while I stood outside, pretty ticked off at myself because I was scared. I've had a problem with being scared of stuff a lot of times.

So, I talked to my counselor, and we made a plan. I argued with my fear. I know that they wouldn't let people ride on it if it wasn't safe. And I know that my friends had a good time on it and didn't get hurt. I don't get sick easily, so I can't think of a real reason to worry about it. So, I promised myself I'd try.

My parents took me back to the park, and my dad said he'd ride with me. Every time I got nervous in line, he reminded me that my feelings were lying to me and told me to ride the wave of nervous feelings (like I learned from my counselor). I'd stop my worried thoughts and remind myself of how proud I'd be when I got off.

Well, I made it! Sure, it was a little scary. But actually it was kind of fun. I'm happy that my nervous thoughts didn't cheat me out of fun this time!

Write one thing you learned from Ahmed about how to face a scary situation.

_____

_____

_____

Rachel Makes the Call!

Hi, I'm Rachel and I'm nine. I'm a bit shy and quiet … and I worry sometimes. My mom is trying to get me to talk to people more and said I could have my friend Kaitlin spend the night this Friday. The problem is she said I had to call her on the phone to ask her. I hate to say it, but I'm nervous doing that.

Mom reminded me to think about what I was scared of. I said I was afraid that she'd say no because she really doesn't like me after all. We held a little discussion about what proof there is that she doesn't like me, and I had to admit there wasn't any. I was at about a 7 out of 10 on my Nervous Thermometer when I called, but I told myself that Kaitlin was my friend. If she said no, it was because she had other plans.

Kaitlin was actually excited and said she had hoped I would call her sometime. She asked her mom, and her mom said they were visiting her grandma's this weekend so she couldn't come. I felt a little sad … but only for a second. Then Kaitlin asked me if I could spend the night at her house next weekend. Cool! I didn't even imagine she'd want me to come over. I'm really glad I called!

Write one thing you learned from Rachel about facing a scary situation.

_____

_____

_____

Take Note

Now write a story about yourself! You may want to have an adult help you.

_____ (your name) **Beats a Scary Situation, Too!**

I am scared of:

_____

What I think might happen:

_____

_____

What is not true about what I think might happen:

_____

_____

What I can tell myself instead as I face my fear:

_____

_____

What I can do if I feel nervous in my body:

_____

_____

NOW, TRY IT!

Activity 33　　　Faith in the Midst of Fear

> **Assignment:** Learn to use your faith or spirituality to help you overcome your worries and nervous feelings.

Many kids believe in God or some type of spiritual power. And for many kids, their faith can be a big help in feeling less worried or afraid.

In this activity, you are to think about your spiritual beliefs and consider how they may help you overcome your worries. Some kids will not want to do this activity, and that's fine. For those who have spiritual values or beliefs, this exercise can help you draw from your faith to fight your fears.

Briefly tell what you believe about God or the spiritual part of your life:

_____

_____

What do you believe about the power of God or your spirituality that helps you in your life?

_____

_____

Do you believe in a power that can protect you or comfort you when you are afraid?

_____

How does this power protect or comfort you?

_____

_____

What can you do to draw from this power of God or your spiritual life when you are afraid or worried?

_____

_____

Is there a minister, priest, rabbi, cleric, or other spiritual person that your parents could let you talk to about your worries? _____If yes, who?

_____

If you have spoken to this person, what did he or she say that can help you with your worries?

_____

_____

How can you help yourself remember to think about this spiritual power when you are nervous?

_____

_____

Take Note

Many kids don't know how much their faith can help them in their lives. When we do our part and let our faith draw from the power of the spiritual or God, we are in good shape for beating our anxiety.

Name one thing that your faith has helped you with before:

_____

_____

_____

Name one thing that your faith is doing to help you with your worries:

_____

_____

_____

Sometimes kids are afraid of the spiritual life and worry about devils or God's punishing them or something like that. Have you ever had those kinds of worries?

_____

_____

_____

And if you did, how did you get your faith to help you worry less instead of more?

_____

_____

If these things still worry you, discuss them with a parent or spiritual leader.

Activity 34   My Success Story

Assignment: Think about how far you have
come in beating your worries.

You are at the end. Hard to believe, isn't it? If things have gone well, you have learned a whole lot about what you worry about, what makes you worry, and how you can beat it. If you have worked this hard to beat your worries, you can be confident that you can face other challenges in life and win!

Imagine there is a newspaper story telling about your success story against worries. Fill in the blanks on the following page to make it YOUR story. You will need to ask your parents for their thoughts in part of this. When you are finished, share it with some people you love. They will be happy about your success, too!

Headline: _____ (your name) **Beats Anxiety!**

_____ (date). _____ (your city). Today

_____ (your name) announced that he/she learned not to let

worry get the best of him or her. _____ (your name) said that

he/she used to be nervous about many things, but the thing that worried him or her

the most was _____. When he or she

began working on this problem with his or her counselor and parents, he/she thought

the program was a _____ idea. _____ (your

name) worked really hard and completed a number of activities. The hardest one of

these was _____.

The person who helped him or her most to stick with it was _____.

It took about _____ weeks to finish, but _____ (your

name) made it through! He or She told our reporter that the thing that was most

helpful in beating his/her worries was _____

_____ (tell what it was).

Now that _____ (your name) worries a lot less, he or she feels

_____ and enjoys _____ much more than

he or she used to.

_____'s (your name) parents said that they felt that their

child had learned _____

during the program and are very proud of him or her. They were surprised at how

well he or she was able to _____.

_____ (your name) was asked what advice he or she would

give to other kids who worry or get nervous at times, and he or she said, " _____

_____."

_____ (your name) told us that he or she knew he or she

would face more nervous feelings in the future, but said when he or she does,

"I bet I won't fret!"

Take Note

As you did this activity, what were your feelings about the program and all the work you put into it?

_____

_____

_____

If you could change the program, what would you change about it?

_____

_____

_____

What about the program do you think was really helpful?

_____

_____

_____

You might go back and look at the Things I Worry About list (pages 13 and 14) you completed. Use a different color pen to mark the ratings you would give now.

Which ones have gotten better? _____

Which ones have gotten worse? _____

What are you planning to do with the free time you have now that you don't worry as much?

_____

ENJOY IT!

> ***Assignment:*** Give yourself credit for doing a great job in completing this workbook!

You can fill out this Graduation Certificate yourself or you can have a parent do it.

You might want to write with a nice pen and make this look really sharp.

Put the certificate up in your room, on the refrigerator, or in another place where you and other people can see it. Every time you look at it, feel good about your hard work and say to yourself, "I bet I won't fret!" the next time a worry comes along!

Do you remember the reward you planned to get when you graduated from the program? Did you earn it? You bet you did!

"I Bet I Won't Fret!" Achievment Award

This certificate is presented to _____
in honor of the hard work and careful thinking
_____ *put into learning not*
to worry too much. Be it known to all who read
these words that _____ *showed*
great patience, courage, and wisdom in doing all the
exercises in the program and in showing that anxiety
can be beaten.

When tempted to worry, _____
can now say with confidence: I BET I WON'T FRET!

Parent Signature

_____ Date _____

Counselor Signature

_____ Date _____

Timothy A. Sisemore, Ph.D., is a child psychologist who has been in practice for 20 years. He has recently focused his work on children with anxiety disorders. Sisemore is professor and dean of clinical activities at the Psychological Studies Institute in Chattanooga and Atlanta, and has published in a variety of media.

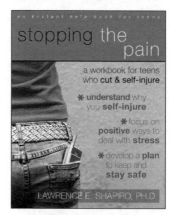